T

"Herukhuti's poetry arrives as a clarion call. Here is an unapologetic blackness firing into the day--21st century, persistent and badass. Listen to a voice heard on the subway, in a lover's ear, in the streets, in the quiet of one's self. Listen, and you will hear the sound of the knife's serrated edge."

- Alexis De Veaux, author of *YABO*

"Straight up Black consciousness before wokeness and critical race theory became buzzwords entering the psyches of those enslaved by whiteness, stupidity, and greed. These lyrical, long-distance javelin jabs pack an Ali punch with all the ferocity of the most agile Black Arts poets participating in raising consciousness like a Sisyphean boulder up the hill of American dumbassification. Herukhuti's *Race. Resistance. Love.* tackles history, race and popular culture with passion, humor and the verve necessary to make us stop in our tracks and pay attention"

- Tony Medina, author of *Death, With Occasional Smiling*

"Herukhuti achieves an artful testimony of community and self while proclaiming an insistent otherness that pushes against historical and philosophical challenges. Between a comprehensive worldview of his own code-switching vernacular and dismantling an all too familiar American paradox, this affirmation of self insists upon anything but surface recognition. All you have to do is listen."

- Carl Hancock Rux, author of *The Baptism*

"I have enthusiastically engaged Herukhuti, times too numerous to count, through conversation, collaboration, and his written work. Not once have I left one of our interactions without new insight, new learning, and a welcomed challenge to my own frame. This collection of poems is no exception. Definitely read it."

- Robyn Ochs, bisexual+ activist and co-editor of *Recognize: The Voices of Bisexual Men*

"Herukhuti is a seer, a bridgemaker and a warrior who vigilantly notices the cusps between worlds. For decades, Herukhuti has opened portals and guided countless seekers through to their highest purpose and now he is offering his poems as portable ceremonies that will now travel beyond the vibrational range of his voice."

- Alexis Pauline Gumbs, author of *DUB: Finding Ceremony*

"Poetry in the language of consent and shared process is a beautiful and magical offering. Through a sharing of words passionately spoken while breathless, Herukhuti has offered us insight into racial injustice, love, sexuality, and Black liberation. Enjoy this exploration of possibility and feel the seeds of joy planted."

- Syrus Marcus Ware, assistant professor, School of the Arts, McMcaster University and co-founder of Black Lives Matter-Canada

"Herukhuti takes us to the past, into the hull of a ship full of our people, and brings us back to the present, all the while predicting a future we dare to consider. *Race. Resistance. Love.* is time travel through the word."

- K. Marshall Green, assistant professor, Williams College and director of communications, Brown Boi Project

"It can be so easy to get seduced by the millions of dollars made off Black bodies and culture and forget what has been sacrificed. That our art and creativity, in all its forms, first and foremost, is the way we have survived, lived, loved, past on our histories and magic; given shape and form to our tears and sorrow and lift to our joys but most importantly, it is the way we have insured that the generations that follow have the tools and audacity to resist. *Race. Resistance. Love.* is a codex for our time and for a time, not too long ago, the impact of which still reverberates today. Cured and perfected over time, the work is the Blues, Gospel, HipHop, Bee-Bop, Trip-Hop; a deep, deep House groove."

- Ifadadefumi Fasnmi Fayemi, artist, educator, activist, healer

RACE.
RESISTANCE.
LOVE.

H. "HERUKHUTI" SHARIF WILLIAMS

A previous version of "Fucked" was published by SisterVision Press in *Ma-Ka Diasporic Juks: Contemporary Writing by Queers of African Descent* edited by Debbie Douglas, Courtnay McFarlane, Makeda Silvera, and Douglas Stewart

A previous version of "Do You Remember?" was published by Vintage Entity Press in *Conjuring Black Funk: Notes on Culture, Sexuality, and Spirituality, Volume 1* by Herukhuti

A previous version of "Add a Dash of Rage" appeared in the film Vale of Cashmere (2005) directed by Sean Drakes

H. "Herukhuti" Sharif Williams

Race. Resistance. Love.

Published by: CCSS Publications, a division of the Center for Culture, Sexuality, and Spirituality sacredsexualities.org

Text Design by: Carlo Diego

Cover Design by: Carlo Diego with Herukhuti

ISBN-13: 978 8 98626 060 0

H. "Herukhuti" Sharif Williams

RACE. RESISTANCE. LOVE.

Acknowledgments

I am grateful to my ancestors, by blood and choice, for growing the foundation upon which I exist and create. Thank you.

I am grateful to the members of my poetic lineage who have inspired me: James Weldon Johnson, Amiri Baraka, June Jordan, Nikki Giovanni, and Sonia Sanchez. Thank you.

I am grateful to the performers and audience members of the artistic community at the Brooklyn Moon Café Open Mic Night in the mid to late 90s. You helped co-create a space for me to grow as a poet and spoken word artist. Thank you.

I am grateful to D. Mingus Harrington. The quality of your work and power of your artistic voice fueled me to get better and better at those open mic nights at the Moon. Going up after you, I knew I had to bring it. Thank you.

I am grateful to the members of cohort 2 of the Digital Evolution and Artist Retention (DEAR) professional development lab of the Caribbean Cultural Center African Diaspora Institute (CCCADI) and everyone who made DEAR a reality. The idea for publishing a book of poetry emerged within me in the community we co-created. Thank you.

Acknowledgments (con't)

I am grateful to Steven G. Fullwood, D. Mingus Harrington, Janessa Waiters, and Gale Jackson for your feedback on drafts of the manuscript and Gariot Louima for your feedback on the layout of the book. Your feedback encouraged and challenged me in substantial ways. Thank you.

I am grateful to Alexis De Veaux, Tony Medina, Carl Hancock Rux, Robyn Ochs, Alexis Pauline Gumbs, Syrus Marcus Ware, K. Marshall Green, and Ifadadefumi Fasnmi Fayemi for reading advanced copies of the book and sharing their thoughts as readers. Your words to future readers are an honor I hope the book lives up to in what it does in the world. Thank you.

I am grateful to Carlo Diego, former student and current colleague, for joining me in this project as graphic designer. Your work was invaluable in the process of making the project a reality. Thank you.

I am grateful to all the readers of my work, people who have purchased my work, and everyone who has gifted my work to someone. Thank you for getting into what I do and amplifying my voice. Thank you.

Table of Contents

Resistance.

Love.

Welcome

This work is over thirty years in the making. Although I have been writing poetry for decades and even published a number of poems, I never thought about publishing a book of poetry until the summer of 2021. My spirituality tells me that everything happens when it is supposed to happen. Until then, I did not call myself a poet. A spoken word artist, sure. But not a poet. I have struggled with embracing any artistic identity for as long as I have known I was creative. Still struggle with it.

I am also a playwright and director. With each of these identities/labels, I have had to do a lot of internal work to claim them publicly. My difficulties in this regard have been compounded by the fact that, in working in academic artistic programs, I have been around a lot of artists with MFAs. That seal of approval has not been mine. I am not an MFA artist. I have learned and developed my craft in community spaces like Maggie L. Walker I. S. 390, the Brooklyn Moon Café, Other Countries, Lambda Literary Foundation's Emerging LGBTQ Voices Fellowship Program, and Third World Newsreel's Video Production Program.

In a society that has made everything marketable and a consumer good, the pedigree I have had as an artist has always made me feel imposter syndrome and insecure about my identity as an artist and, by extension, my artistic work. Even in the face of praise and positive feedback. But I am also someone who loves the hot shit whether it be produced by someone else or me. And while all of that insecurity is true, I have also felt great about creative work that I've produced that is *fire*. So I hope you find that in this project.

I play with form in this book in several ways. For example, "The Day They Put Beyoncé to Rest" is a contrapuntal poem meant to be read as one poem or two separate poems. "Conclusion" is a found poem that is purposely not named in the table of contents, so it appears hidden in the book. I created it out of an investigator's conclusion in response to claims made by faculty colleagues racialized as white that I was harassing them when I called them out for being racist or through my professional engagement with them, which left them feeling embarrassed by the way they appeared in those interactions. "Can a Love" is an original song with my social critiques written as editorial comments on the page. I also asked the graphic designer, Carlo Diego, to play with the layout of the work. But much of this work was originally written to be performed for audiences rather than to be read by them. Not being constrained by the knowledge and limitations that an MFA background would have placed on me, I also did not have the pressures to conform to particular discourses about poetry and poetic forms when I wrote the work in this book. As a result, the poems contained within appear as I have felt them appear to and in my mind-body-spirit-soul.

Content for me, as a poet and reader of poetry, is just as important as form. I believe in the aesthetic philosophies of Nina Simone and Toni Cade Bambara, who said that the artist's duty is to reflect the times and to make revolution irresistible, respectively. Creative and exciting forms don't move me if they aren't used to express meaningful experiences, emotions, physical sensations, and/or ideas. The themes of this book—race, resistance, and love—are the result of me reading over decades of poems I've written, reflecting upon over forty years of living a revolutionary, counter-hegemonic life in opposition to settler-colonial, imperialist, white supremacist, capitalist cisheteropatriarchy, and recognizing how my poetry reflects the life I've lived.

RACE.

Ezekiel 37

Da bones
  dey dere in dat sea, in dat great big ocean deep
dey lay dere and dey make da ground shake
dey insides add to and mix with da salt of da sea
dey da bones of does dat would not be what da white man wanted
dem to be

Da bones
  strong as rock, would rather sit in mother ocean den be crushed
by white man's world

Do you know about dee ocean?
do you know she power?
huh?
what you know if you don't know dee power of dee ocean?
she is mother
see?
Olokun
Yemoya
Auset
ya understand?

Dem bones jump into her
dey jump into dem Mother.

(laugh)

Dem jump right into dee belly of dem Mother
dey buried in her womb
dey back home in her belly

No, dey aint dead!
what dead?
No dead in dee belly of dee Mother.

(pause)

Dey dere waitin
dey dere in da belly of dee Mother waitin   waitin come back
dey aint finished with da story yet

(laugh)

Why I laffin?

(pause)
Five hundred million dem out dere
waitin   waitin
knowin and waitin
da story aint over yet

(laugh)

Five hundred million dem out dere
alive   waitin   knowin
and waitin
da story aint over yet

Dem out dere no integrationist or separatist
no democrat or republican
no capitalist or socialist
dem out dere is African
African and angry
alive
knowing and waitin
five hundred million bones hard as rock

What ya tink dey gonna do when dey come out from She belly?

No

Da story aint over just yet.

(laugh)

The Noose

Twisted racial histories
Knotted,
Cancerous and umbilical
Nurturing us on a diet of hatred and fear
Tugging, tugging, tugging each time we move forward in our evolution
Through multicultural contact and cross cultural communication
Reminding us where the boundaries have been drawn
That boundaries have been drawn
That drawn boundaries have been crossed
Danger ties the knot, murder tightens the loop

Rope used to pen other animals
Keep them from getting away from masters and owners
And their defined roles as personal, private property

Get back, darkie
Get back, blackie
Get back, you uppity nigger
Get back

How easy it seems for the fibrous material to become stone
Atoms congeal and rigidly align to form a heavy weight
Crushing everything in its path
Easy, it seems

Appearing, ghosting, and reappearing
Ulcerated afterbirth hung in public
Signaling the arrival of a still born
Carried well past the ripening season
Ready to be buried
If only we had the will

Black bodies swinging from trees
Stripped of clothing and life, bleeding from
Places where flesh and organs once existed
Intimate places seen only by mothers and lovers

A noose reclaimed
Decades after the expiration date
As symbol and signal
Of the consequences of trespassing and transgression
Grandchildren reach for what was never grand about their grandparents

Cellular memory transports us in time
We are back when families brought picnic lunches
To the spectacle
While other families grieved and trembled with powerlessness
A loved one became the next one
To exhaust breathe against the rope
Go taut at the end of the torture

It is amazing how efficiently we can pull from that past
Archetypal sirens maroon us on harsh racial shores
With names that we dare not speak
At least not in polite, professional conversations
Yet if we look through the loop and past the knot

Along the path we find the whippings, amputations,
Castrations, and plantation tortures
Replaced by the bare noose
A.E. and B.O.
After Emancipation and before Obama
The new ways we inscribe time
To help us believe in a selective past

Where we find the noose
Gives us much to consider
At work and school
Desegregation's battleground states
Places of intimate social contact
Finding the noose in these spaces
Places where we earn a living and earn access
There's no coincidence
No clearer message
There is no right to living
No right of access
For the darker brother
Even as he is brother, sister, friend, lover,
Coworker, student, mother, father, boss,
Employee, human
Being.

Cosmos Inspired

Jazz musicians and prophets
sit and talk
about the progress
of the work,
the work in progress.

Man, the human condition
the hue man condition.
Maaaaaaan, the condition of the hue man.

Don't let the rhythm hit 'em;
let it move them into the part,
part of the whole.

I scream, you scream
we all scream
when God screams
as blood pours out the ears
from the magnanimity of the dot.

A love supreme, a love supreme.
A love supreme, a love supreme.
Now the sax.

Give me a B flat and F sharp
enough to cut through all
the bullshit, horseshit
eagleshit, ratshit.

That's it, that's it.
Hear the drum, beat it.
There it goes, on and on...

And now, back. Back to Black.
Glad to be back. Glad to be Black.
Glad to be back
Black.

Hear my call, hear my call
AT&T, T-Mobile, or Verizon,
No, a sprint's not good enough for the speed of thought

And a 1 and a 2.
Turn 360° infinitely on the spot.
Too tough to box with God;
Arms too short, minds too caught.

Give praise.

Do You Remember?

do you remember what they told us they told us
you are having sex with everyone he ever had sex with
and you wondered why the sex didn't feel better last longer
with all these other motherfuckers in the picture

do you remember do you remember do you remember what they
told us what they told us what they told us they told us
the consistent and proper use of a condom drastically reduces
your risk
of HIV infection
a latex sleeve reduced our sexual risk
while we could be jailed for the sex we were having
our sex was pathologized demonized ostracized our sex was filled
with self-hatred guilt shame objectification envy and rage they
called that safe
how the fuck is a condom going to protect you from a nigga that
hates himself
and hates you for loving him how's a condom going to protect you
from wanting that motherfucker's dick
up in you in the first place

do you remember do you remember do you remember what they
told us what they told us what they told us they told us
HIV is the virus that causes AIDS
yet they had no causes
only correlates
they made the AIDS definition and infected HIV with it

said HIV causes AIDS what about the cause of HIV where'd that come from
why did it come at that time
did they tell you
green monkeys Africans Haitians were targeted
but did you find the answers where are the answers now

do you remember do you remember do you remember what they told us what they told us what they told us they told us
AIDS is the leading cause of death among... AIDS is leading the cause of death
like Martin Luther King or Farrakhan leading marches on Washington
like Caesar Chavez working for economic social justice in the fields
like Sojourner Truth and Harriet Tubman working for women's rights and human rights like complex Angela D
struggling against the prison industry
AIDS is a freedom fighter leading the cause of death

do you remember do you remember do you remember what they told us what they told us what they told us

they told us
AIDS equals Death
and thousands of people
who passed third grade math prepared to die
so many people got ready to die of AIDS
there wasn't enough preparation to live with HIV
T cells got higher viewer ratings
than the Cosby Show and Cheers combined
T cells went up and down more than park trade
on a dick at 2 am

do you remember do you remember do you remember what they
told us what they told us what they told us they told us
only immediate family may be present
and we were discarded along with precious pieces of people
we loved as family
cared for as family
when family was neither immediate nor familial

do you remember do you remember do you remember what they
told us what they told us what they told us they told us

he has 3-6 months to live
and they tried to get us to stuff a life
into the container of one moment
one action

do you remember do you remember do you remember what they
told us what they told us what they told us they told us
here are your test results and we were scared shitless
because there was that one time
I knew I shouldn't, but that nigga had me open
and he looked ok he was clean didn't have any
cuts bruises open sores swollen nodes or glands scaly skin drawn
cheeks
blotchy spots really low muscle mass

do you remember do you remember do you remember what they
told us what they told us what they told us they told us
your test came back positive and life stopped
and started again

all our worst fears became true
we wept
on our knees and the floor
fetal knees pressed against our beating hearts
But we lived and we died but we lived and we died but we lived and we died

do you remember what they told us what they told us

what they told us

Lessons I Learned by 4th Grade: Beatitudes

Blessed are those who dance, play, and love
for their souls will be filled with beauty.

Blessed are those who fight to open doors
for they shall see tomorrow.

Blessed are those who give care
for they shall blot out isolation and fear.

Blessed are those who rip ferociously through the flesh of subjugation
for they shall always be satisfied.

Blessed are those who seek truth
for they shall survive the pitfalls of ignorance.

Blessed are those who organize in the darkness
for they will know the joy of accomplishment.

The Day They Put

I was there the day they put Beyoncé to rest

Black girls had to be something other than fierce and hippy
white girls had to wrestle with a different kind of beauty

I was there the day they put Beyoncé to rest

The gay boys lamented with wails and shrieks worthy of a Queen
Though it was the faggots who said that music suffered not

I was there the day they put Beyoncé to rest

Radio, music TV, and recorded sound recreated itself
While lyrical skill, musicianship were resurrected from their lost graves

I was there the day they put Beyoncé to rest

No one pondered Jay Z's marital status
Because its relevance became instantaneously obsolete

I was there the day they put Beyoncé to rest

She appeared as choreographed and packaged as ever
Yet no longer commanding the usual adoration

I was there the day they put Beyoncé to rest

People lined the streets throwing liner sheets
But corporate moguls remained unbothered

I was there the day they put Beyoncé to rest

Chile, it seemed her end started as destiny
However painful it may have been for some

Beyoncé to Rest

Not the girl from Houston who met Selena
Dreaming of being her one day

The child more familiar with studios or rehearsals
Than classrooms and play time

The person standing in the elevator
Watching her sister go upside her man head

The woman who fears and cries, wants and tires
Feeling the loneliness with so many people around

The woman navigating work thinking
Like a man and acting like a Queen

No, not She who isn't accessible to view or stream
Make into a thought piece on feminism, or make viral

They didn't put her to rest because
She was not ever theirs

I Am

I am looking for love's lasting embrace while cradling the soothing
satisfaction of my purpose
I wonder how fear rests so deeply in one's heart that paralysis is
the only response
I hear the crying of souls waiting to feel freedom's mission
I see babies wink with anticipation entering the world
with change on their lips
I want to pay attention to the tender things with family and friends
I am looking for love's lasting embrace while cradling the soothing
satisfaction of my purpose

I pretend to be domesticated so that the fearful won't have reason
to fight or flee
I feel exhausted at all the work masking involves
I touch lavender to the lips and speak elegantly to the cautious
I worry about how much truth they can handle or when their
bough might break
I cry the suffering and shed tears into the breach
I am looking for love's lasting embrace while cradling the soothing
satisfaction of my purpose

I understand that tomorrow brings the renewal of dreams deferred
I say yes to a future I help to create
I dream to feed and water that future
I try to listen closely and remember the wisdom revealed
I hope to see as much of that wisdom's labor realized
I am looking for love's lasting embrace while cradling the soothing
satisfaction of my purpose

Untitled

Balance is justice
justice is rightness
rightness is happiness
happiness is peace
peace is stability
stability is knowledge
knowledge is creativity

in the abstract
things flow
on and on
because there's no alternative
what is, is
what was, was
what will be, will be

so give to the dance
if you drum, then drum
if you sing, then sing
if you dance, then dance
now is the time
for the chorus

back to the center
where the dot becomes

larger than the circle
circle expands to encompass existence

existence becomes real
then, the innerspection

in the valley
we look for nothing
and find everything
because the oracles were right

silly fools sit and dally
around an idea that
stretches consistency
into a chasm of sometimes
overrun villages in Kyoma
call to the sisters for relief
and feel the pain of outside influences

allow the maximum effort
to flow from top down
giving sunshine to the peoples
and the opportunity for greatness
among the youth

CONCLUSION

The evidence supports that the witnesses who participated in this investigation experience Williams as ~~divisive. They describe a pattern of behavior in which he responds to criticism, whether real or imagined, with contempt. He calls people racist - even likens them to plantation masters - as a way to demean and silence those who challenge him or his ideas. The witnesses interviewed for this report shared a similar experience of Williams and all were affected negatively by his behavior toward them.~~

~~Based on the limited facts uncovered in the interviews and without the ability to engage in an open-ended interview in person with Williams, the undersigned cannot conclude that Williams' behavior and conduct are motivated by the recipient's membership in a protected class. Rather, the evidence suggests that Williams' behavior is motivated by sensitivity to perceived challenges or comments that he interprets as racist or stemming from white supremacy.~~

~~All of the witnesses interviewed for this investigation credibly reported experiencing distress related to their experiences with Williams. They came to dread working with him or attending meetings with him. They found him unpleasant and unkind. However, the evidence is insufficient to establish that Williams' conduct was motivated by or based on these employees' protected class, rather than on his worldview and his experience as~~ a Black man ~~and that the behavior was severe enough and persistent enough to result~~ in a hostile or abusive workplace. ~~Without sufficient evidence of~~ both of these elements, the offensive and disrespectful behavior ~~does not~~ rise to the level of prohibited harassment.

Respectfully submitted,

Ellen Coogan

Ellen M. Coogan **aka KAREN OF ALL KARENS**

RESISTANCE.

To Live

To live
with a clear mind
undisturbed by the madness, the
    sadness, the egoness of
    a myth come to some kinda reality

To live
is the very isness of
    I am
the creative union of a Soular
functioning

To live
and be in the irreducible
fashion of existence and feel
    the smooth soothing rhythms
of a correctness that is not
promoted by the cynics from
the conglomerate

To live
in the it is I, and
    not question whether
to be or not to be
but rather when to be and
    when to be even more

Call it the to live thing
to be thing   to I thing
          but don't call it too late
not when the hum
of the drum is dumb
call it
call it,   as, during, and while
call it   before, because, and be there

To live
not the impossible dream
but the predestined dream
the unquestioned dream
because being in the to live
conjures dreams into reality
and the illusion of non-existence
lasts only in the minds of
the ignorant, for even
the dead have the ability

To live

Ode to My Lover

truth
truth is an assfucker
i can't remember
all the times i bent over
backwards for truth
let truth slide right on in
truth has opened me up
many a time
and put a smile on my face
i met truth a long long time ago
i first started out letting
truth cum in my mouth
i would caress truth with my tongue and
let truth roll
off it
truth don't care about whether you're ready or not
truth will get in your ass in a minute
it'll hurt
may even
be some blood
but truth always gives you what you need
i've known truth for a long long time
truth's not into scat
so don't come with the bullshit
truth likes it real
truth will give it to you
real

some people
like to play with truth
like to tease truth
like to manipulate truth
or so they think
but they don't know
i've been with truth a long long time
ya don't fuck with truth
i've learnt that the hard way
truth is not to be played with
teased or even bent
truth is straight up in your face
or ass
truth will leave you
if you don't give respect
for what truth has to offer
truth will let you in
to explore truth's insides
yeah truth flows that way
truth will open up to you
as long as you're open to truth
that's what's meant by
truth is relative
relative meaning versatile
truth gives and receives
truth goes both ways
truth has been with me for a long long time
and in that time
i've learnt one valuable lesson

truth'll set you free

On the Inside

Inside my heart
Sadness, regret, and loss of innocence
Working the earth in painful indifference
Struggling for self-nourishment
Strides wide, labored
Traveling brings experience and tears.
When I die my body will find rest in the bellies of worms,
While my spirit finds another door, another day.
I remember youth, my youth
I remember struggle, confusion, loneliness, and conflict
I remember being young meant to be unfinished
Now I only wonder
what next
And I can only be right now
Where we gather, we share wounds
Where we are together, we feel a part
Tears don't flow easily for those who respect the hurt
Tears become libation to another scar
Still asking
Why did I do that
Where did that come from
How did I let that happen
What went wrong that time
When will it get better
Still saying
If I could've
If I had just
If I had've only

If I was able to
My hearts pounds a beat
of sadness, regret, and a loss of innocence
Tasting the sweat of each day's labor
and the blood of each day's wounds
Smelling the stench of each day's death
and the mildew of each day's deeds
I look to my end when the gray of my hair
will add to the gray sea of my fathers and grandfathers.
Let my flesh drop from my bones
so that it can be food for my sons.
They, too, will learn the dance and
be eaten by their work, by their hurt,
by their deeds, by their sons
Let the universe behold
it needs my heart
filled as it is with
sadness, regret, and a loss of innocence
Being a son of Devils makes being young acidic
and being old TBD
Being a son of Gods makes me vulnerable
and wounded.

Dixie. Is We Somebody?

Dixie was a plantation baby
Raised on milk from a Black Mamadonna
Her alabaster skin nourished on ebony gold
Learned how to digest African flesh when she got older
Akan, Yoruba, Igbo, Wolof, Mandé and Chamba

Dixie has had so many Black men in her (women too)
Jealously held them close
Even built Angola and Parchman walls
To press them tight between her thighs
Forcing them to find relief
By escaping under the protection of the night shade
Hands up, don't shoot is as old as Cartwright said niggas were crazy
For wanting to be free.

Dixie' a mean bitch
She will never forget that they left her
But can't seem to remember the reasons why
She denies the whippings
Lynchings
Cross burnings
The scared children in the other room crying
Their tears glistening to the torchlights outside
Fueled by savage rage and white hunger

I want to justifiably homicide Dixie
But I am a man (Black if you ask the wrong people)
You call me sexist; her hands have been tightening around my neck

Four hundred years
I can't breathe
You ask me to spare her feelings

I want to pick up some form of justice
And smash her across the country with it
Cause skittles shouldn't be covered in blood
Bike rides shouldn't precede police rides that end
In death
And toy guns shouldn't be invitations to the morgue

My head's caught between her legs and she's pressing me
Closer and closer to her snatch
I smell cotton fields and swamplands
Red clay and watermelons
Strange fruit and burnt crosses
Sweaty bodies and lynching trees
Smiling faces and fear

If she takes me in and I end up dead, I want you to know
I did not commit suicide
Trying to kill Dixie
Will you help me?
Stand up against your fear
Like Fanon told you
Decolonization is alwalys violent
So somebody's got to die
Be hurt in the process
Even if it's a metaphorical death
A death of Naiveté, Dixie's mulatto cousin

Her standing in the way of progress; asking Dixie, is we sick?
Yes, Dixie is sick.
The doctor said she had psychopathic racial personality
Can't be cured with no penicillin
Even if you're in Tuskegee
Dixie is alive and well. You ever wonder why there ain't too many Black women named Dixie?
Not even Dolezal Black
She ran away from Dixie too
Didn't like her as a friend, sister, mother, auntie or grandma
But Dixie tried to keep her
Get our help to hold her down and swallow her whiteness whole
But she wouldn't do it
Didn't like the taste, smell, feel, sound, look of Dixie
No relations, that's what she told us
Not even a distant cousin

Like
Dixie Carter
Dixie Chicks
Dixie Cup, holds the blood of Black people every 28 days
Fort Dix
Fort Bragg
Fort Campbell
Fort Hood
Fort Benning too
Damn, I didn't realize there were so many soldiers hiding up in Dixie
Did you?
So many of them too.
With guns and shit.

Weapons of mass disruption

Ready to kill a nigga or niggress

If we allow them

And we keep allowing them

Keep bending over backwards

For the foot, heel, baton, chokehold, bullet

Ain't somebody gonna kill that Dixie?

Is we somebody?

Is we?

The Kiss

ever take a moment
to appreciate the beauty,
the awe-inspiring beauty
of a kiss?
not
the casual or quickie kiss
given to someone
on the fly or when there's nothing more to say.
the kiss that says more, does more
than words could ever convey

when desire wrests itself free
cascades from the heart cavity
lips part to release
breath previously trapped by possibility
whispers lust's secret into the space
between lovers
and need builds a bridge that curiosity
planned a long time ago.

what is it that draws the tongue
into the open mouth of another?
calls it to take up residence
lavishly.
its new home plays host
pampering and providing
all that could be imagined
and more.

the kiss
open-mouthed, tongues intertwined
full lipped and deeply meaningful
is such a beautiful contraption.
whether observing or participating
there is no escape from the
transfixing nature of a good kiss.

palate hollow forms a retreat
for the tongue desperate with longing
desire swims
thrashes against flesh
moist and cool
while heat rises from lusty loins
and breath pauses to collect itself
in a chest overcome by the driven
rhythm of heart.

it is amazing how much
of oneself can be pushed
into another
through a mouth
yearning and available.
the kiss reminds us that
love, lust, and desire
are consuming
and must be digested properly.
no need for knives and forks
when thick lips and supple tongues
work around and over each other.

did you learn to kiss
like you learned to pray
eyes closed, yearning to be filled
bathed in spirit washing over
your tensed body?
fellowship in the ecstasy
making sacred profane
and profane so damn
sacred that tears drip
down questioning cheeks while mouths
move in unison
salty elixir mixing with
the mouth's nectar.

taste the ingredients
of a well lived life.
project your tongue further;
intrude upon the moment
that mouth was born
and every moment since
until destinies merge
into the very moment
of this kiss
breath extending
passion filled
honest, wholly honest
finally,

forever

Add a Dash of Rage

Chambers of rage and violence
hold a private place for the Fanonian drives
the anti-social person's actualities

I hunger to crush a skull
to rake skin off flesh
frozen from the shock, horror
of a beast unleashed, finally and ready

Hearing the deep umph of a tightened fist hitting
That beguiling sound called Just-us/Justice

Violence and rage, rage and violence
disrupt slumber
shake the civilized from the safety of their cribs

I can hear the rattle of a skirmish unfolding
and I love every minute, moment, Movement
There's no place for ballet

when the heat is up and there's bodies

To free

Can't you feel the soothing warmth of anger
how it takes the chill off tired, broken bones

Give me that ole tyme religion of rage and violence
Let us look into each other's eyes

No more fake smiles

Hidden gestures or mumbled insults
Let us do unto others
right in their faces

With the most complete and fullest expression
of rage as is violently possible

It would make us all feel a lot better
in the end

Photograph

It was there on Ocean's blog
The photograph
Of Bill
Playing the flute while taking oxygen
June 2007
Mount Sinai Medical Center

It was there in that photograph
Of the photographer
That Bill
Became thousands of words for me
Years of memories
An artist who was his art

It was there in that photograph
That Bill
Showed me
What he had been doing for years
With his art
Using cold technology to express spirit

It was there in that photograph
That his art and medium
Became clear
Camera used to tell a story
Humanity's story
Transplanted thru the lens, Bill's lens

It was there in that photograph
I remembered
Bill at Black Funk
Nude body among bodies
Forming yoga
And brotherhood and one of humanity's chapbooks
It was there in that photograph
Bill's calves
Came to mind
Those huge, beautiful calves
I feared
The feel of them behind a kick

It was there in that photograph
Kinky Bill
Peeked behind the air tube
Raunchy and sexy, musky sweet
Cannabis-scent
Nurturing another orgasm

It was there in that photograph
Bill used
The air that technology fed him
To make music
Proving again the artist's mission
To make art, no matter what

Sex without Ceremony

let me put my dick in your mouth

let me feel the inside of your cheeks along my shaft
without a discussion of morality or religious conviction
no holy admonition or ethical rebuke

let me put my dick in your mouth

give it a bath in your mouth
without considering genetic predisposition
no pc talk just you and me

let me put my dick in your mouth

slowly draw it through your lips as your moan vibrates through me
ignoring that your eyes are shaped different than mine
or maybe your skin's hue doesn't imitate mine

let me put my dick in your mouth

let me feel your tongue play soothing waterbed
I don't want to hear confessions of penis envy
no feelings of shame as I see your dick harden

let me put my dick in your mouth

take lollipop sucks on the head
without congressional approval
no official sanction from rome, mecca, or biblebelt, usa

let me put my dick in your mouth

press my balls close to my body
oblivious to eternal damnation
just dick, lips, tongue, and throat

let me put my dick in your mouth

suck me in deeper as my cum drives through me into you
let's enjoy such simple things, together
kiss me with my cum and let me sample my flavor

Fucked

I got fucked last night
Not by some thick-ass chocolate honey
taking off her tighter-than-tight jeans
oh so brilliantly revealing her elaborate frame
licking red red lips that sorta roll out from her face
to meet and greet the most fortunate seeker
I didn't have the pleasure of her company,
her eyes, her tongue moving moaning in my mouth
her smell pouring from her flesh
her ass calling my hand to hold it, squeeze it
pull it, her taste or rather the taste of her
the taste of her neck, her breasts, her thighs
her toes, her pussy
I can't speak of feeling
the feeling of her soul cradling my soul
in good, in special, in now, in blue
ya see none of that happened
But I got fucked last night
Not by some crème-cocoa nigga with that fly-ass curly hair
his deep brown sly eyes only betraying the secrecy of his appetite
to those who know what to look for
body by God, design by Gym
hands smooth but large, knowing where to touch
why to touch
looking at me stealthily and wetting his lips with that tongue
that bewitching tongue
We didn't retreat to some dark place
away from the eyes, the stares, the assumptions, the conclusions

to lie down, licking each other's wounds
loving and lying, lying and loving
goatee-clad face against mine
bronze-stained dick against my ebony meat
No I wasn't stroking/getting stroked by a brother-lover
Getting fucked ain't always that pleasurable
but I got fucked last night
Someone's child went to bed hungry, sick, and alone
They got fucked, I got fucked, we got fucked
Another human being took the being out of another human
They got fucked, I got fucked, we got fucked
Prison walls struggled to muffle the wail of a million tortured souls
They got fucked, I got fucked, we got fucked
Trees celebrating their 500th year on earth got overturned by a
  10-year-old front loader
They got fucked, I got fucked, we got fucked
Skulls of seals are cracked open so that coats of elites look plush
They got fucked, I got fucked, we got fucked
Pregnant mothers sucked on glass dicks while 13-year-old
  daughters did tricks
They got fucked, I got fucked, we got fucked
Children were burned by bombs and bitten by bullets
They got fucked, I got fucked, we got fucked
Food poisoned and water polluted
They got fucked, I got fucked, we got fucked
Sometimes getting fucked means getting fucked over
And strapping on a condom ain't enough protection
When you don't know
you me them us
are really getting fucked

LOVE

Ma

Wounded young woman,
Loving her Black child so much,
Fears remembering

Moved

laughing with friends and comrades
i saw her move sandalwood fragrance into the room
wearing a shimmering emerald radiance
that hugged everyone she passed
and tugged ever so slightly at your attention

had to notice her
not in the everyday sense
it was more like
when she entered the room
her presence made you realize
how empty the room had been before her

her warmth, melting me away
she knew her power, i could tell
it was evident in the way she walked
the floor was something
she needed for longer than the few moments
her feet graced it

don't get me wrong, she didn't move fast
she just moved, and moved

then she did the unthinkable
urgently i cursed/praised my widening eyes
as she
smiled
not just with lips and teeth

no
this woman, angel, demon
had the nerve to smile with her whole body

that was it for me
what else could i do, she was
disarming,
hell, she was dismembering me
breaking me up into little pieces of promise

so i turned away, closed my eyes
i knew i would have only one chance
let myself feel what she was doing to me
every one of my cells vibrating

slowly i turned, opened my eyes
before i saw her again, i felt she
receiving my signal
our eyes formed a relationship
before our lips could make excuses
and at that moment, i knew
motion

Choosing

I remember when my beating heart
Pressed emptiness around me
Making solitary gestures
Far removed from melancholy;
Faint, abstract memory of before him.

When did spooning,
His back against my chest
Ass against dick
Chocolate nuzzling amber,
Become so essential to life?

We found each other,
Bodies encountered each other,
Hearts matched each other.
Before him became the past;
My present formed next to his.

Sympathetic responses
Ripple through my body.
Necessary scares me.
I remain connected however;
Choosing the present
Over before him.

Can A Love

Verse 1
You just left and I'm lying here
Don't know why I still seem to care
But every time you put that stuff next to me
I know there's no way I'll ever be free

Verse 2
Angry at myself for not demanding more
I've acted like I don't know the score
If I keep myself small this way for you
I know in my heart this is all you'll ever do

Chorus
Can a love do more than have you grinning in bed
Can a love do more than mess with your head
Can a love be the life that you have with someone
Can a love be the work that you make sure gets done

Bridge
I'm getting out of this bed and thinking with this head
So I can create the love I know is there in my heart

Verse 3
Every path to love starts with one step
I'll find my way to where love's kept

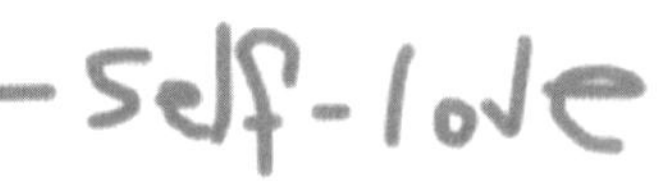

No need for anger or resentment at you
People love you the way you show them to

Chorus

Can a love do more than have you grinning in bed

Can a love do more than mess with your head

Can a love be the life that you have with someone

Can a love be the work that you make sure gets done

Goodbye 2 Fuck Boys

Hostile Mama

hostile mama

holding hungry

boychild

holding empty

bottle

holding

emp

ti

ness

while a tired, old song

plays over and over

on a broken, inconsolable record player

it skips and fits

through gospel

then blues

she hears the cries

the crying

of the child

as the chorus

of the song

her hatred

and anger

fool her

senses

again

when she looks

at him

her eyes

focus

on the man

not the child

and she

remembers

how the blood

felt

coming from her

nose

how the eye

closed

and the world

was dismembered

so she lifts him

the child

like she wanted

to lift him

the man

off of her

and she

throws him

the child

like she wanted

to throw him

the man

the thump

against the wall

skips the record

the last chorus

heard

no more

Standing There Looking Good

Unworthy feelings pressed my fears
Against the rhythms of desire.
I come unaware
Shame has taken residence in the slim crevices of your mind
Craving out
A way to find pleasure
Value in another man's body.
Heart assaults me
Breath leaves me
I am the lip that your tongue slowly traces
Afraid
Excited
I want to be everything that you are
Climb inside your body
Swallow down what you appear to be
Feel the velvet warmth of you enveloping me.
'Cause, damn nigga, you look good
Only means I think you are the man I'm not.
Reflections of the mind
Don't stop the blood from flowing to gorge flesh
Erection laden thoughts
Blow lust and passion into ears
Before bodies touch
Trying to man up
While quivering against the confirmation
Of
Who we are
Who we are not

Who we want to be
Will never be.
Two feet away and hemispheres apart
We hold ourselves at bay
Remaining the nigga I should be, while denying the nigga I am
I refuse you, and myself.
Can't get my head around
How to love him
Or me
Fully
So I settle for what's left
Retreat to the safety of everyday shit
Doing our thing for the one millionth time
No big deal, we know this shit
Nutting
Zipping up and leaving out
Making the trip back tomorrow
So that time never produces
More than what we're comfortable swallowing
And we never have to do any more than
Stand there looking good
Knowing there's more to being a man
Than doing a man.

Bitch's Brew

Stink and flow bitch
send that musky red/brown seepage into my mouth
send it spilling in globs of discarded flesh
making glop glop glopping sounds of gravity-controlled eruptions
i want to smell the earthy stench of your meaty pit of hair and flesh
mucus and blood and blood and blood
as i breathe in the natural aroma of your syrupy bayou,
choke against the pressure and heat
the gaping wet hole between your legs
i shudder under its blanket
covering me from the inside and from the out
leaving me no space to relieve myself of the intensity
i drink in the promise of
prevent my soul from asphyxiation
salty, vile nectar invades my mouth
sending shock waves through me
burning my throat, stomach burning
the bitch's brew makes a cauldron of my gut
i feel her stirring her concoction of cunt with sous chef pride
she enables me a moment to settle into my fate
i am filled
with the spirits of an unholy ghost
served in a wicked black rose glass
dry, no ice
then she dances
with it dripping onto the floor
with it dripping
and on the floor

with a dripping floor

drops splatter

leaving meaningful memories of misery

pain, violence, decay, of death

be not proud death

not a shroud but another drop

her poison nectar hitting the weather worn wood

as she dances

i can't hold onto it anymore

i feel her brew bubbling out me

seeping like sweat through virgin pores

i add to the mess on the floor

i have become a part of her chemistry

looking down into a pool of my own private poison

order another round, and this time

make mine a double

Bigg Mike

How do you take back a moment
Sever it from time
Burn it up until there's nothing left
Make it gone never happened non-existent
I can see him there
In the darkness of that moment
Rage and fear playing with each other
Pressed up against his chest
Beating down the heat
Crashing against his gut
Choking him at the waist
While blood runs down
A chef's knife
The news labeled it a butcher's

Mike came from culinary school
To my place where
We had sex bound in rope
Embraced each other to sleep
Watched movies
Teased the other to laughter
Yes, there were lies
And a kind of love that meant something
Even though that something was not
Enough

Did he go to the theater
To fill a space where I was absent
Finding less than a bed and no love
I can feel him resisting the advances
Of poisoned intentions and misguided eyes
Hands on his slight frame
I wonder did the darkness of the moment
Push him against a wall
Marked no escape

He cut through his aggressor
Into a prison cell
Held together by 15 years and regret
How would the world be different
If he chose something different
Somewhere different
Someone different
Somehow different

How do you take back a moment
Sever it from time
Burn it up until there's nothing left
Make it gone never happened
Non-existent

I want different for him
I want him finishing school
Cooking in a kitchen
Making someone laugh
It doesn't have to be me

I didn't want it to be me
But I can't help feel sorrow
For the person who shared my bed

Fetishes, desires, my semen even
Took me into his self willingly
Makes me wonder if I am incarcerated with him
A piece of me residing in him
From our time together
Residing in a personal part of the penal and punishment system
What am I to do
My responsibilities to him to myself
Just found out today
My feelings followed behind the news
Clumsy and lost
Until they met me sitting in a chair
About to cry and calling for help

How do you take back a moment
Sever it from time
Burn it up until there's nothing left
Make it gone never happened
Non-existent

I Found Love on My Way to Joy

I cried to joy last night
I cried and cried
Seeking a truer picture of me

Tears flowed from the corners of my eyes
Never stopping until I got to joy
Joy was a place to get to

The journey there was made of pure feeling
As the tears poured, I felt closer to me
Closer to joy

My tears fell to the earth
Becoming the footprints
Marking my journey

Before I knew it
In a moment of stillness,
I emerged

And so today
If I seem different
Just know

That last night
I made it to joy
And found a lover in me

H. "Herukhuti" Sharif Williams, PhD, aka Dr. Herukhuti (all pronouns) is a revolutionary and decolonial artist/cultural worker, cultural critic, and public intellectual whose work examines the impact of settler-colonialism, imperialism, white supremacy, capitalism, and cisheteropatriarchy on people across ethnic and racial differences. They are a playwright, stage director, documentary filmmaker, performance artist, essayist, and poet. Dr. Herukhuti is the award-winning author of the experimental book *Conjuring Black Funk: Notes on Culture, Sexuality, and Spirituality, Volume 1* and co-editor of the Lambda Literary Award nonfiction finalist anthology and Bisexual Book Awards nonfiction and anthology winner, *Recognize: The Voices of Bisexual Men.*

Dr. Herukhuti is a member of the artist collective No Homo | No Hetero, which refers to being neither homosexual nor heterosexual. NH|NH is an umbrella organization and organizing principle behind a collection of projects and activities designed to promote the healing, growth, and general well-being of sexually fluid, bisexual identifying, and bi+ men of African descent and their communities. Envisioned as a multi stakeholder cooperative with an emergent approach and philosophy, NH|NH seeks to elevate, educate, celebrate and when necessary interrogate notions of manhood, masculinity, power, love, relationship and community utilizing various artistic and indigenous African cultural practices. Understanding the need for safe, supportive, liberatory spaces, NH|NH seeks to cooperatively provide resources and opportunities to build and sustain communities.

An experienced educator, she has worked with hundreds of students around the world to engage in transformative learning for social justice. Dr. Herukhuti is a core faculty member in the BFA in socially engaged art, co-founder and core faculty member in the decolonial sexuality studies program at Goddard College and adjunct associate professor of applied theatre research in the School of Professional Studies at the City University of New York. He is the founder and chief erotics officer of the Center for Culture, Sexuality, and Spirituality, a social enterprise dedicated to revolutionary change through the use of the arts, embodiment, and indigenous knowledge traditions from Africa, Asia, and the Americas.

Dr. Herukhuti lives with a drapetomania diagnosis which causes life affirming experiences and life threatening episodes as well as career suicidality.